Alfred's
Premier Pian...

REPERTOIRE BOOK 1

MW01131618

Dennis Alexander, Gayle Kowalchyk, E. L. Lancaster, Victoria McArthur & Martha Mier

FOREWORD

Alfred's *Premier Piano Express Repertoire, Book 1* includes motivational music in a variety of styles, reinforcing concepts introduced in *Premier Piano Express, Book 1*. The pieces (including one duet) in this book correlate page by page with the materials in *Premier Piano Express*. They should be assigned according to the instructions in the upper-right corner of each page of the book.

All music was composed or arranged by Dennis Alexander and Martha Mier. The music in this book can be used as supplementary repertoire for any method. Students will enjoy performing these pieces for family and friends in a formal recital or on special occasions.

ONLINE ACCESS INCLUDED

🔊 **Audio Performances and Orchestrated Accompaniments**

TNT³ Practice Software

To access the audio and software, visit:
alfred.com/redeem

Enter this code:
00-48630_228822

CONTENTS

Copyright © 2019 Alfred Music
All rights reserved. Produced in USA.

ISBN-10: 1-4706-4340-5
ISBN-13: 978-1-4706-4340-9

Alfred

alfred.com

Cover Images:
Piano photo courtesy of Yamaha Corporation • Stack of paper image © Getty Images

2

Use with Premier Piano Express, Book 1, Unit 4, page 35.

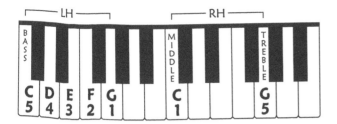

My Best Friend 🔊1

Dennis Alexander
Martha Mier

Duet: Student plays one octave higher.

Use with Unit 5, page 37.

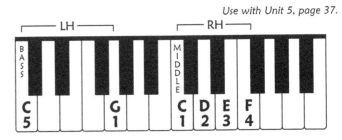

Backyard Camp-Out 🔊 2

Dennis Alexander
Martha Mier

Gently

Move down

Play one octave lower – – – ⌐

Gently
Both hands 8va

The Movies 🔊 3

Dennis Alexander
Martha Mier

Duet: Student plays one octave higher.

Use with Unit 6, page 44.

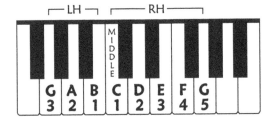

Mulberry Bush 🔊 4

Arr. Dennis Alexander
Martha Mier

Happy waltz tempo

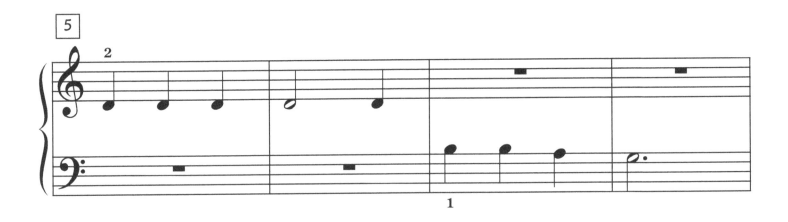

Duet: Student plays one octave higher.

Happy waltz tempo

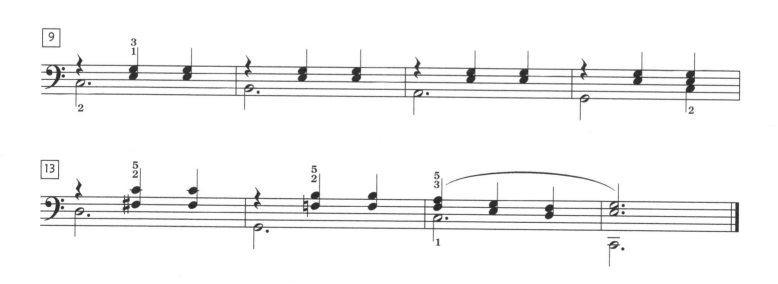

Use with Unit 6, page 45.

Starlight  5

Dennis Alexander
Martha Mier

Gently

Duet: Student plays one octave higher.

Anvil Chorus  6

(from *Il Trovatore*)

Guiseppe Verdi (1813–1901)
Arr. Dennis Alexander
Martha Mier

Stately

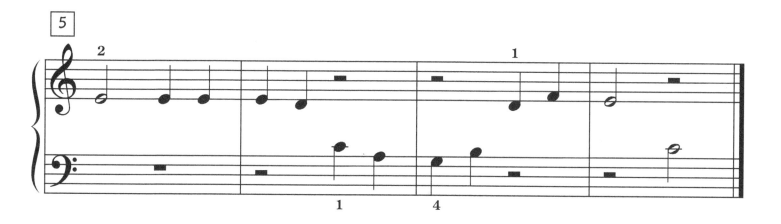

Duet: Student plays one octave higher.

Use with Unit 6, page 47.

The Boat Dock 🔊 7

Dennis Alexander
Martha Mier

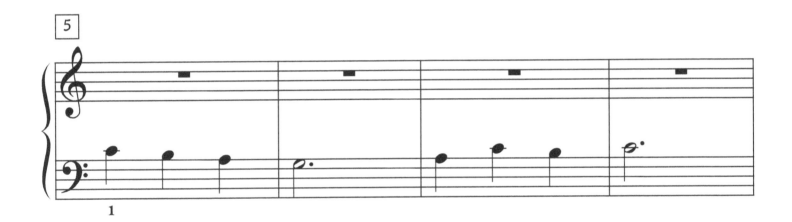

Duet: Student plays one octave higher.

Use with Unit 6, pages 48–49.

Opening Day  8

Dennis Alexander
Martha Mier

Duet: Student plays one octave higher.

Green Tea

Dennis Alexander
Martha Mier

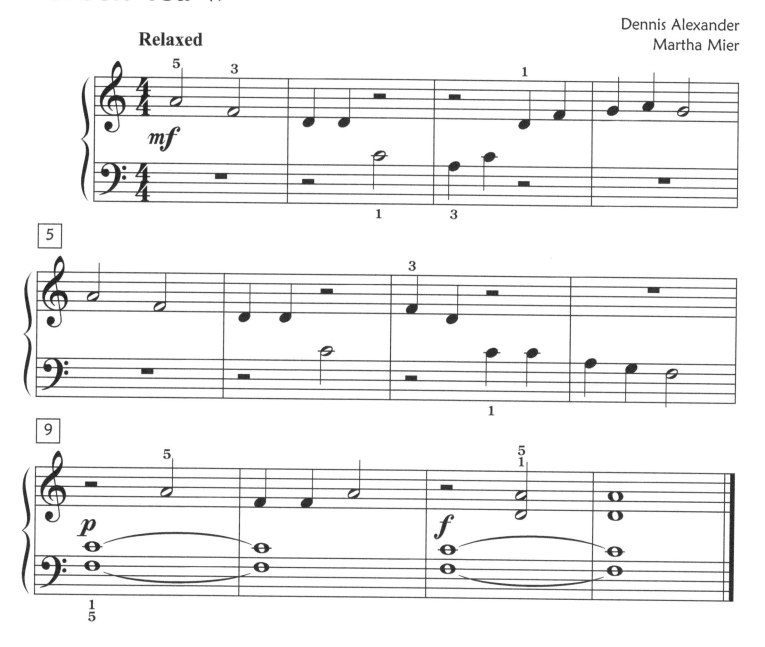

Duet: Student plays one octave higher.

14

Use with Unit 7, page 52.

Time to Celebrate 🔊 10

Dennis Alexander
Martha Mier

Duet: Student plays one octave higher.

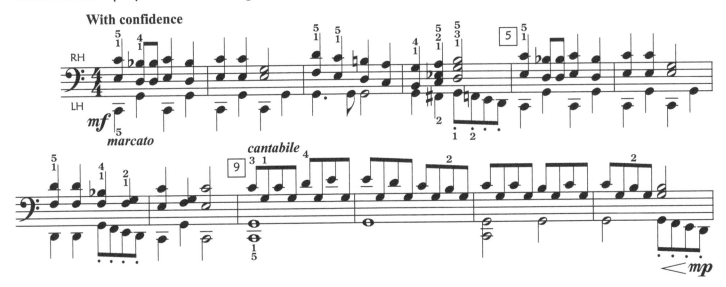

Use with Unit 7, pages 56–57.

Drum Circle

Secondo

Dennis Alexander

Drum Circle

Primo

Dennis Alexander

Lively

Both hands one octave higher than written throughout

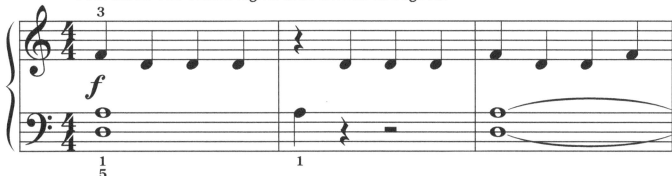

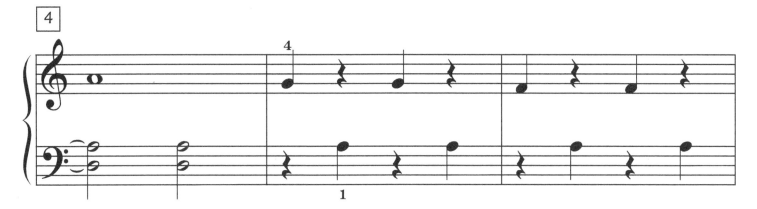

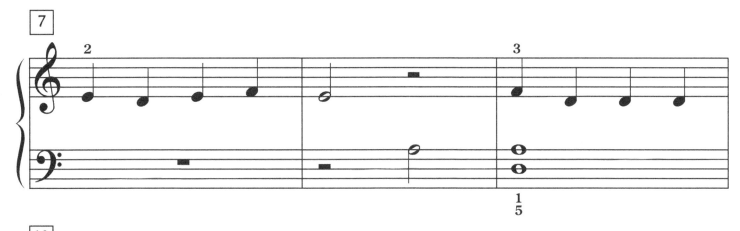

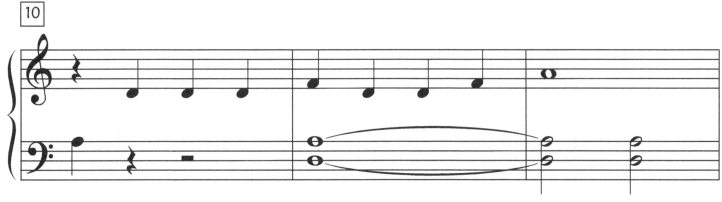

Secondo

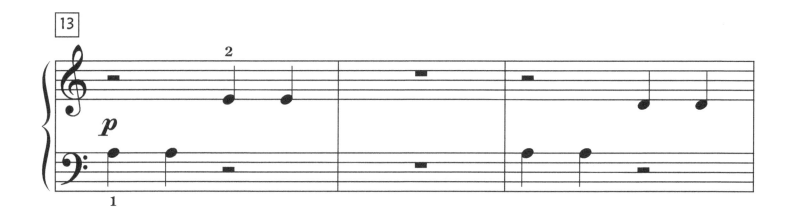

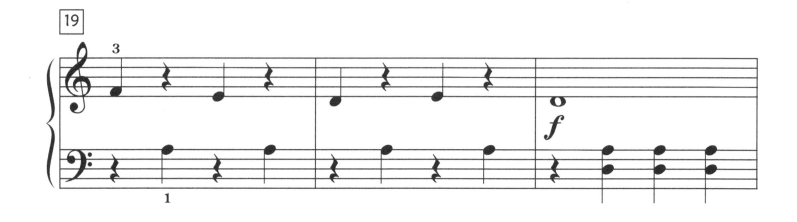

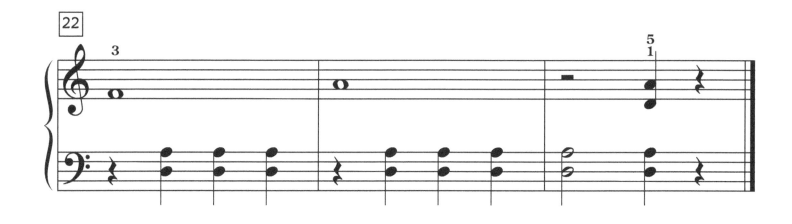

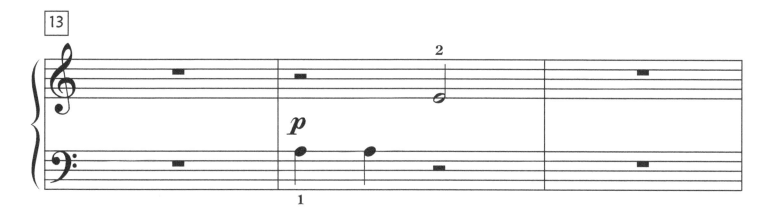

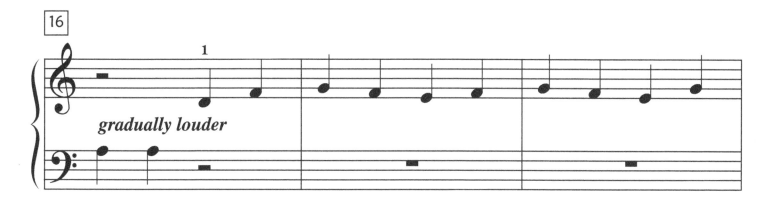

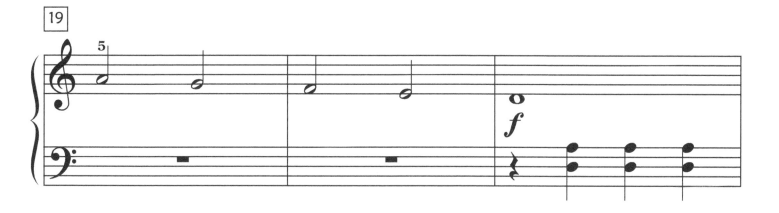

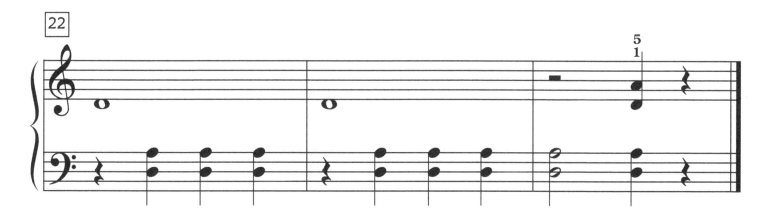

Use with Unit 8, page 61.

Scottish Shortbread

Secondo

Crisply

Martha Mier

Both hands one octave lower than written throughout

Press damper pedal and hold to end.

Scottish Shortbread
Primo

Martha Mier

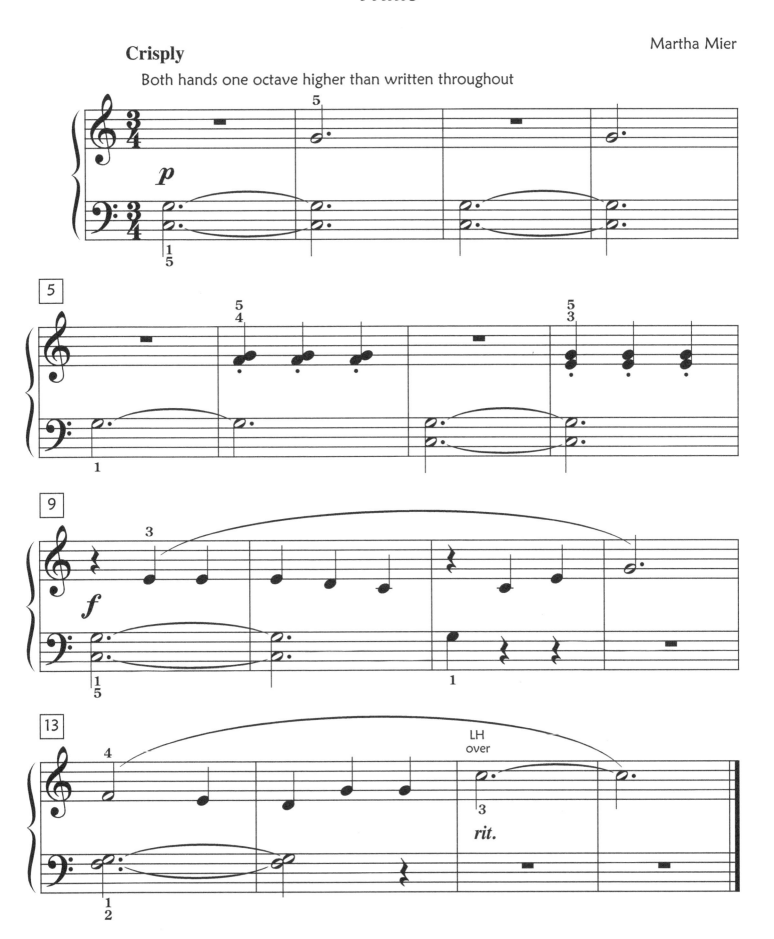

Use with Unit 8, page 66.

Good Night Waltz

Dennis Alexander
Martha Mier

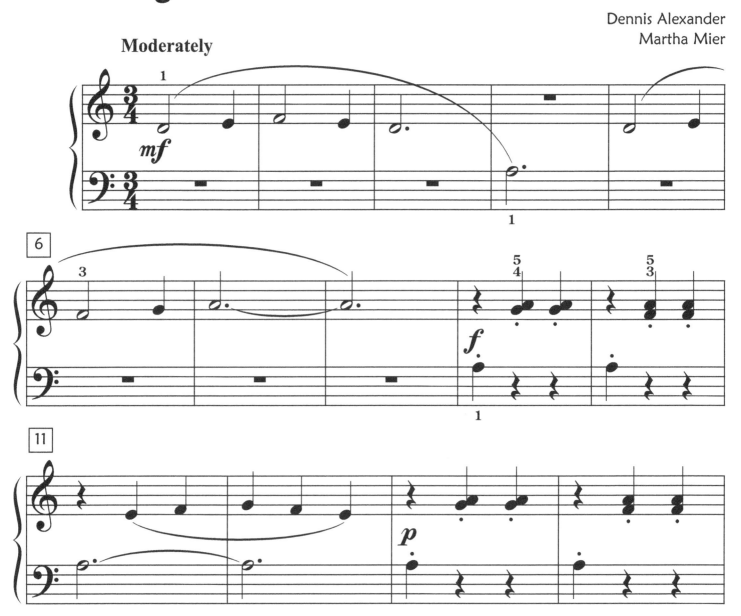

Duet: Student plays one octave higher.

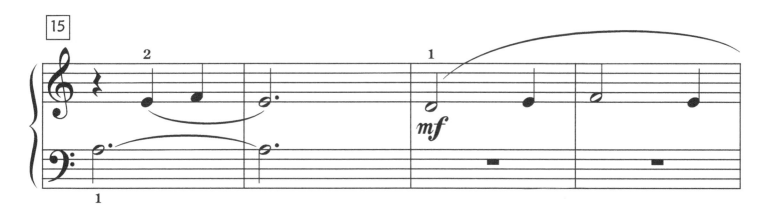

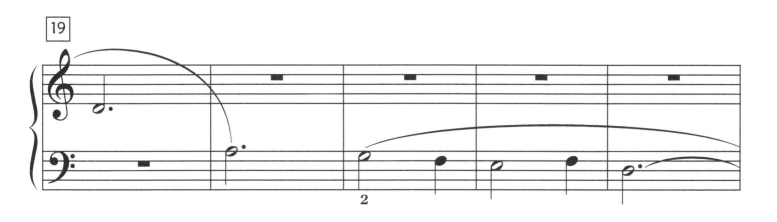

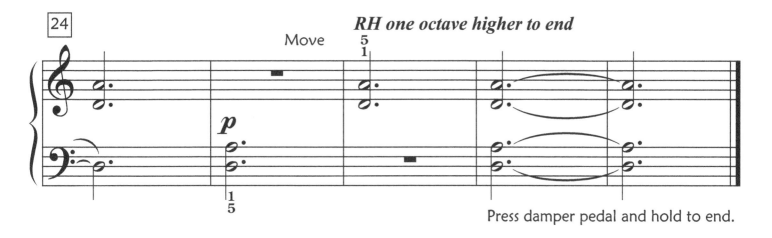

Move

RH one octave higher to end

p

Press damper pedal and hold to end.

Use with Unit 9, page 75.

I Just Love Pizzazz!

Dennis Alexander
Martha Mier

Duet: Student plays one octave higher.

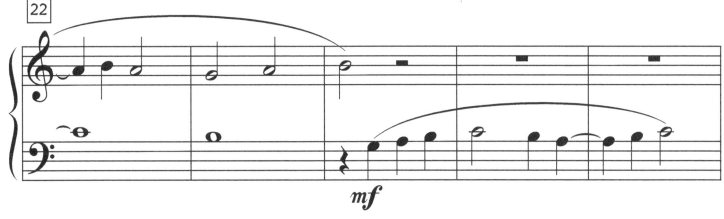

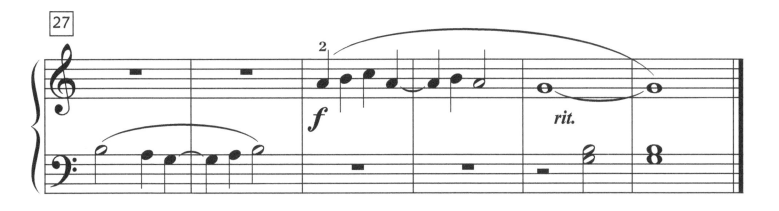

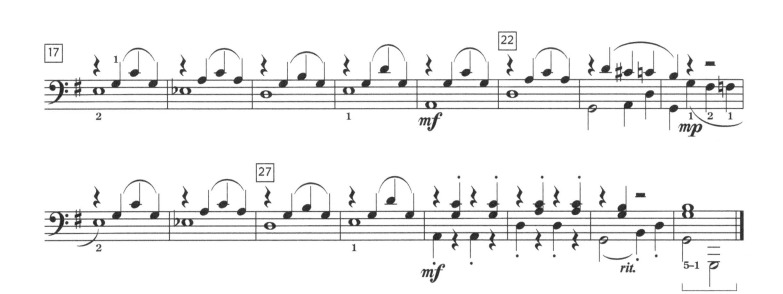

Use with Unit 10, page 83.

Scottish Plaid 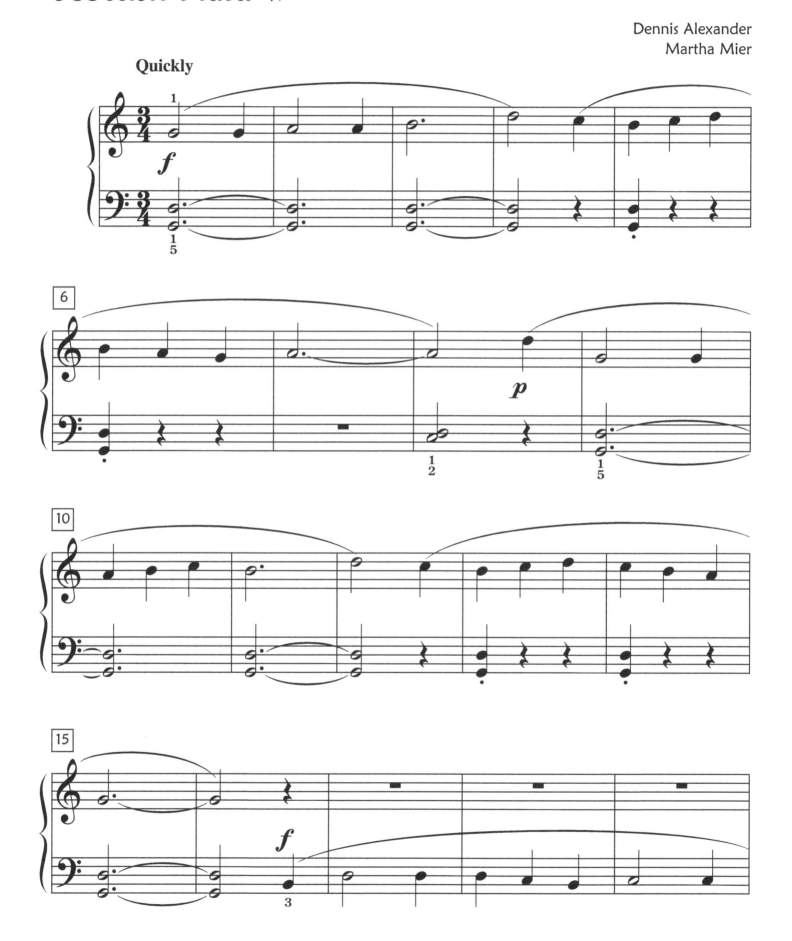 12

Dennis Alexander
Martha Mier

Move RH up

8va -

p

Press damper pedal and hold to end.

Use with Unit 11, pages 88–89.

I Love to Play Piano! 🔊 13

Dennis Alexander
Martha Mier

Fast and rhythmic

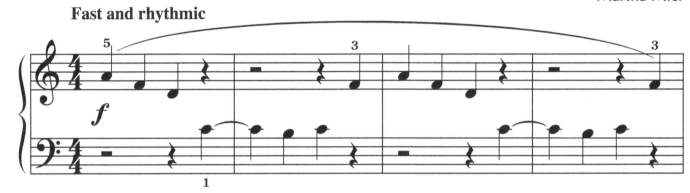

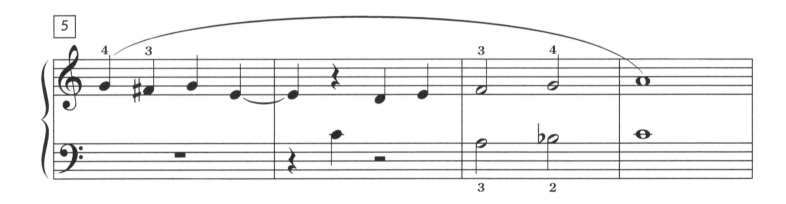

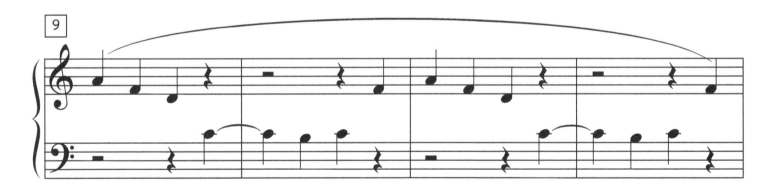

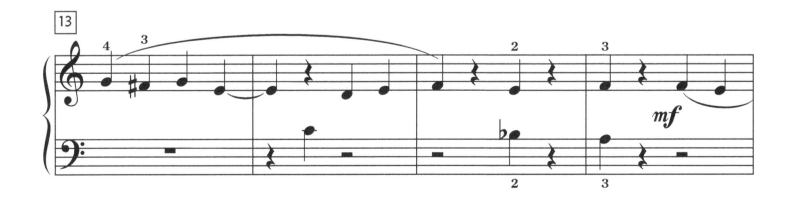

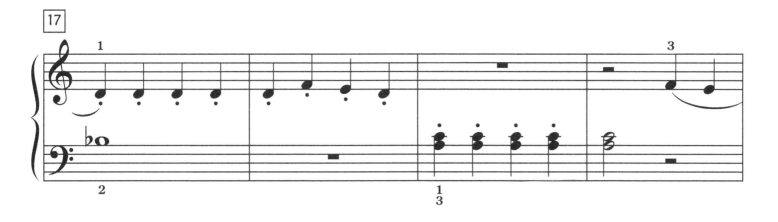

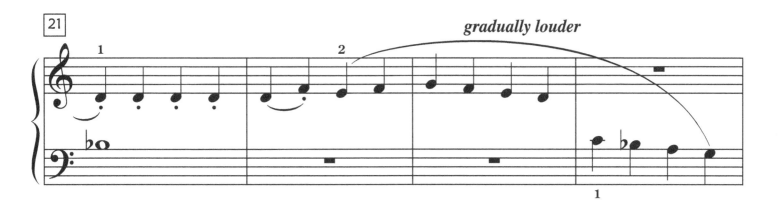

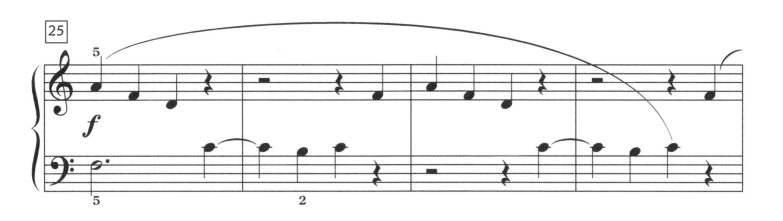

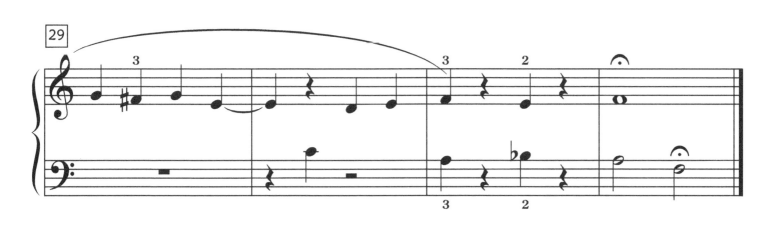

Use with Unit 11, pages 94–96.

At the Skating Rink

Dennis Alexander
Martha Mier

Duet: Student plays one octave higher.

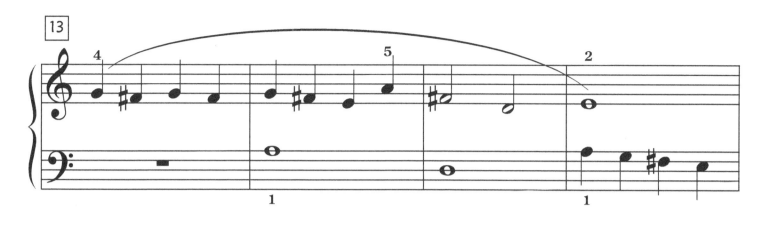

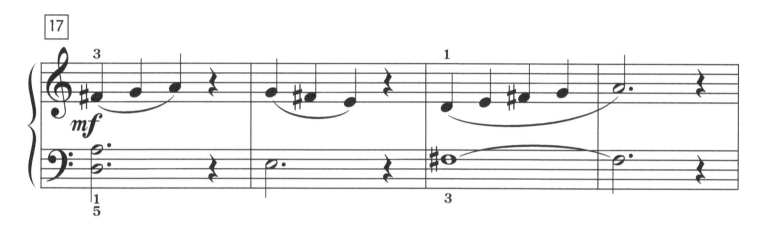

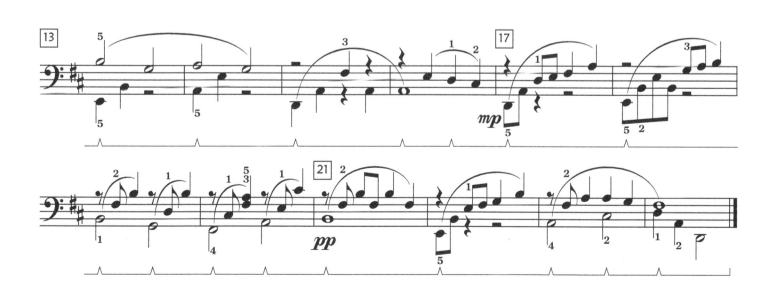

Audio Performances and Accompaniments

Stream or download audio performances on acoustic piano and orchestrated accompaniments for selected pieces in the book. Identified by a speaker icon (🔊) with a track number next to the title in the book, each selected piece includes four versions of audio:

- An acoustic piano performance at **performance tempo**.
- An acoustic piano performance at **practice tempo**.
- A digitally orchestrated accompaniment **with** piano.
- A digitally orchestrated accompaniment **without** piano.

Practice Software

For a more versatile practice experience, download the TNT 2 practice software, which allows the user to adjust the tempo of each track. Check the included Read-Me file for system requirements and installation instructions.